PISTE

THE COMPLETE SKIER

Distributed by:
SAANNES Publications Limited
Box 6209, Station A
Toronto 1, CANADA

Publisher:
OTTAWA SPORTS PUBLICATIONS LIMITED
1755 Fisher Avenue
OTTAWA, Ontario, K2C 1Y1

PISTE

by Douglas Godlington
and Christopher Reynard

THE AUTHORS

CHRIS REYNARD has for many years been running the Weekend Ski Club and taking countless hundreds of skiers to experience the perils and frustrations of skiing.

DOUG GODLINGTON, as well as being an artist, is also a ski instructor—which is worse, for it is his sort that cause most of the suffering in this world.

FOREWORD

SKIING. Two weeks of glorious sunshine. Two weeks of wonderful bracing mountain air, of speed and exhilaration, and the complete satisfaction of racing effortlessly down through vast fields of virgin snow. Always in complete control. If we believe all those glossy brochures, this could indeed be us.

On the other hand, it is much more likely that we shall arrive at our resort and find that there has been no snow for four weeks. Bare patches will tear the soles of our skis to shreds, not to mention those numerous sharp rocks that appear from nowhere at the exact point at which one's bottom is destined to land.

Never mind, the snow will probably start to fall quite soon after we arrive. And it does—non stop for the next ten days. So much for our two weeks of glorious sunshine!

As for the speed and exhilaration—this will probably amount to careering down the slopes completely out of control, and landing painfully first on one side and then on the other at intervals of about 25 yards. It is likely our safety bindings are not adjusted properly and will release in the middle of our first perfect snowplough turn, or else will obstinately remain shut when we collide with our exasperated ski instructor for the umpteenth time.

The queue for the ski lift will, in all certainty, be so long that the end of it is only a short distance from the beginning of the run. This being the case, we shall have to resort to tramping uphill each time we wish to perform yet another wretched stem-christie with skis crossed and finishing in the usual painful heap at the bottom. All this to the general amusement of the rest of the class.

The joy of dancing effortlessly down through a field of moguls may be roughly translated in the lay skier's language as: hitting the first bump (or mogul) too fast, attempting a turn in mid-air, hitting the second mogul with crossed skis, taking off again at even greater speed and with even less control, missing the next two moguls completely and hitting the fifth one with such a force that the resultant three and a half backward somersaults with spiral twist takes us quickly to the bottom of the run, ready for our next attempt.

Our experience of those marvellous and unending fields of virgin snow will probably amount to a quick *schuss*, followed by an abortive attempt at an *avalement* turn with ski tips a good three feet below the surface, resulting of course, in the biggest jumble of skis, sticks, legs and arms imaginable; not to mention the acute discomfort of having that lovely soft snow right down our backs, filling our pockets, and getting into every conceivable nook and cranny. Then comes the problem of picking ourselves up. After repeated attempts at pushing ourselves on to our feet with a ski stick that continually disappears into the bottomless depths below, we shall probably have to resort to taking our skis off and making our way down the mountain on foot. The chair lift by this time of course will have closed for the night.

And so we return to our hotel; tired, weary, aching from every limb, bruised, frustrated, and thoroughly chastened—vowing that never again will we attempt such a ridiculous 'sport'.

And yet, next morning at the crack of dawn, with some strange compulsion which we cannot understand, we shall again set off for the slopes with our skis on our shoulders. Day after painful day, frustration after frustration, hoping all the while that sometime soon we shall emerge into the brilliant sunshine and ski with the effortless grace of all those fabulous skiers we watch so often on television.

The process continues from week to week, from holiday to holiday.

Your authors, have suffered too. And in our suffering we have done many hours of careful research into how skiing can be enjoyed without the accompanying tears and frustrations.

We have pioneered the very latest in ski equipment, to ensure the maximum comfort and the optimum skiing success. Further, we have devised a foolproof method of skiing technique, so that even the greenest of beginners can become a Jean-Claude Killy after only a few easy lessons.

And we have investigated carefully the most successful psychological approaches to skiing, so that even if one can't ski, one can at least give friends the impression that one is a name to be remembered in the skiing world.

Chapter One: SKI EQUIPMENT

IF ONE WERE to take a census of all skiers to find out how many skied without suffering any discomfort, pain, or worse, one would probably discover only a tiny percentage. And these would be viewed with extreme suspicion by the remainder.

If one were to look up the definition of masochist in the dictionary one would surely find some reference to skiing. How many times do we see skiers hobbling painfully from the slopes with dislocated knees, pulled ligaments, torn muscles, bruises, sprained ankles?; how many times do we see cases of frostbite and exposure?; how many times do we see skiers walking along bare-footed in the snow carrying their ski boots?

We even heard of one skier who, without exaggeration, had pieces of sorbo rubber tied around every part of his body by bits of string!

Now this would be enough to deter *any* beginner from ever taking up the sport. We feel that the time has come to give skiers a better deal, give them some of the little comforts of life, so that skiing might even become a pleasure. Skiers have been hampered too long by equipment which demands a certain ability and effort on the part of the skier, and have been subjected to discomforts from which more sophisticated equipment could free them forever. So, starting overleaf, are our suggestions for the future of skiing.

Equipment can normally be a fairly expensive item; however, if you follow our suggestions religiously, it need only cost you a small fortune.

COMPUTER CONTROLLED SKI BOOTS
Can be programmed for different types of ski turns.
(In the popular price range, at around $13,000).

PUNCH CARD

COMPUTER

ACTION OF
COMPUTER STEERING
MECHANISM

PERFECT SNOWPLOUGH

IMMACULATE
STEM CHRISTIES

RELAXED AUTO-PARALLELS

FAULTLESS
AUTOMATIC
WEDELN

PROGRAMMING FAULT-
CATCHES EDGE

PAIN OPERATED
SAFETY BINDINGS
Release when an impulse is received from the
brain registering pain. Operates through small
electro-magnetic cell $9,750.

SKI SUIT
Thermostatically controlled one-piece, incorporating ski mitts and socks, for maintaining constant body temperature.

GOGGLES
Complete with windscreen wipers, screen washers, and demisters.

SKI HELMET

Complete with yellow flashing beacon for use in 'white out', and siren for warning other skiers of their impending doom.

RADAR

For detecting other skiers in 'white out'.

**ARTIFICIAL SNOW
MAKING DEVICE**
For continual powder snow skiing. Not to
be used while stationary . . .

SONIC DEPTH DETECTOR
For testing depth of powder snow.

LASER BEAM
For turning ice into spring snow.

PERISCOPE
For skiing in deep powder snow

WOW!

**THIS BOOK
IS HOPEFULLY
DEDICATED TO:**

ALL WOULD-BE SKIERS WHO WON'T
and
ALL COULD-BE SKIERS WHO CAN'T

INFRA-RED SUNRAY LAMP
For obtaining bronzed Alpine complexion.

CASSETTE TAPE RECORDER
For skiing to beautiful Alpine music.

TWO-WAY RADIO
For obtaining assistance.

...AND COFFEE WITH TWO SUGARS.

PERSONAL VIDEO TAPE
For admiring own technique.

TELESCOPIC/BINOCULAR SKI STICKS

For use in big moguls . . . and closer scrutiny of attractive German Fraülein.

MATE DEVICE
For luring attractive German Fraülein into head-on collision.

ANTI-MATE DEVICE
For clearing the way on crowded pistes.

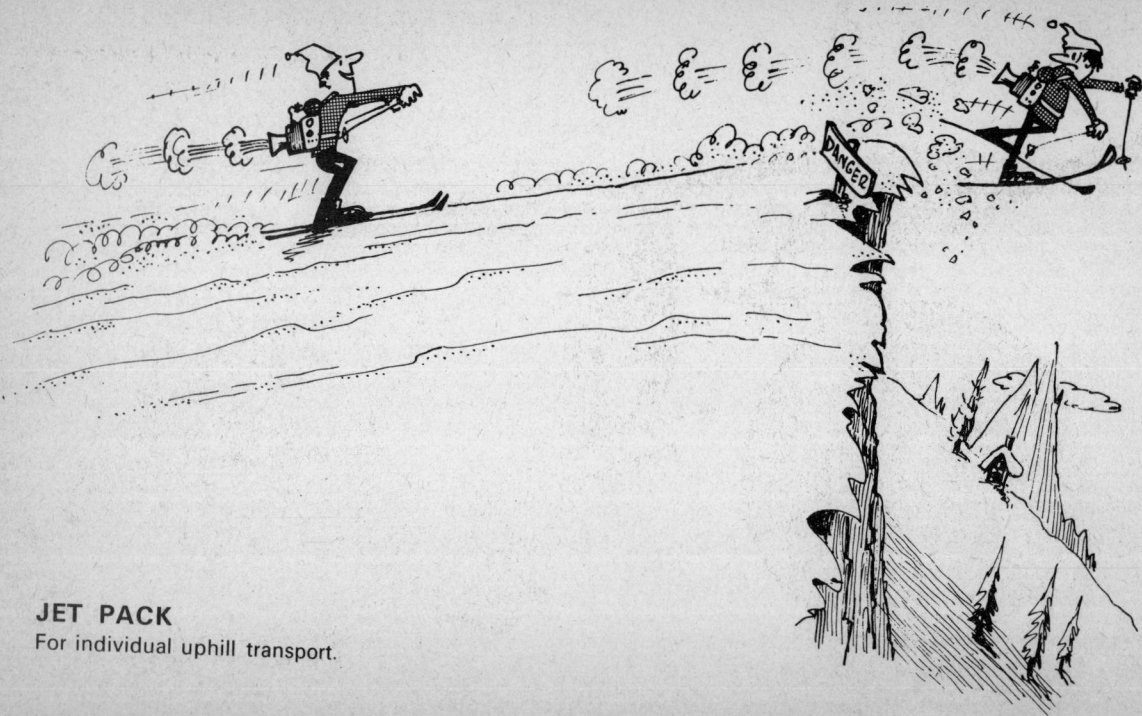

JET PACK
For individual uphill transport.

SKI JETS
For emergency change of direction.

BOTH JETS NOT TO BE
USED SIMULTANEOUSLY!

PARACHUTE
For emergency stop.

HEAVY MACHINE GUN
For detecting avalanche danger.

COLT 65 REVOLVER
For administering first aid.

SPRAINED FINGER

DRIP FEED
For Glühwein transfusion.

SURVIVAL KIT
Consists of tent, blankets, food, TV, etc.

SNOWPLOUGH

N.N.E.- VEERING

65 M.P.H.

NIL

DISASTER!

METHOD OF TURNING

DIRECTION

SPEED

TECHNIQUE

PROSPECT

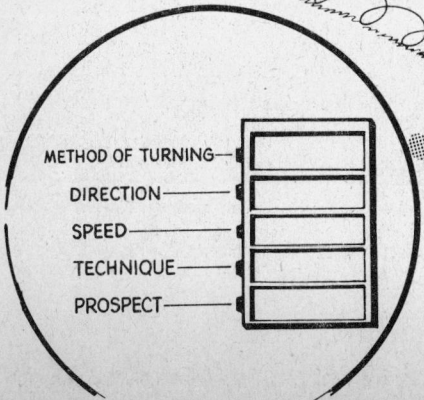

INFORMATION CENTRE
To give other skiers their prospects of survival.

BAYONET
For jumping ski lift queues.

SLALOM GATE SHIFTER
Retractable arm from side of ski to move slalom poles into impossible positions for following racers.

SLALOM COURSE RUTTING IRONS
Snow scoops fitted to backs of skis to create huge ruts, making life more difficult for those behind.

INFLATABLE BOTTOM PROTECTOR
For happy landings!

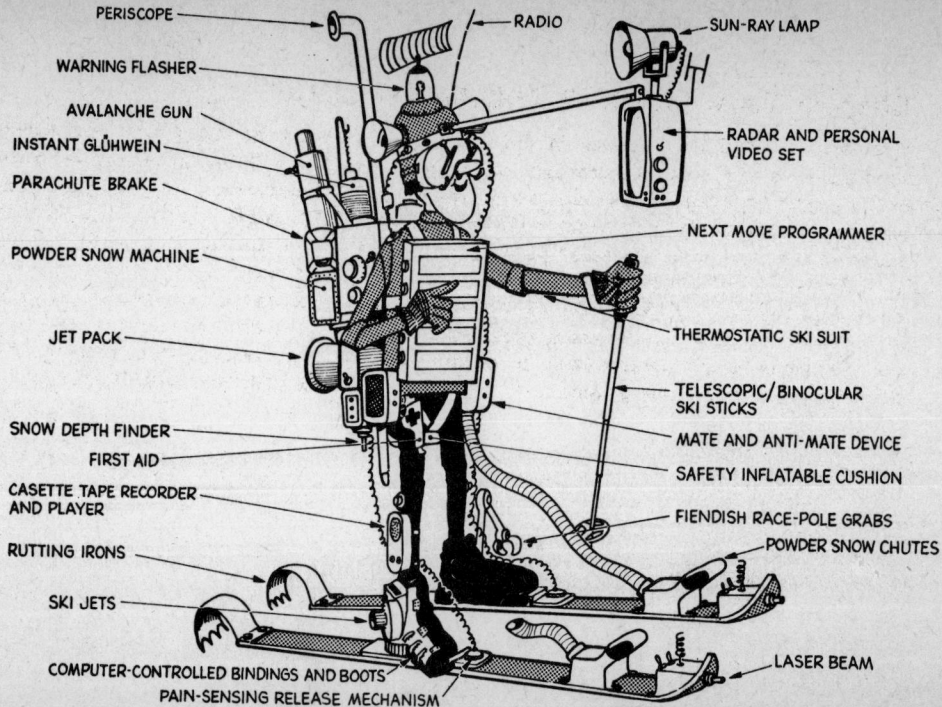

THE COMPLETE SKIER

- PERISCOPE
- RADIO
- SUN-RAY LAMP
- WARNING FLASHER
- AVALANCHE GUN
- INSTANT GLÜHWEIN
- PARACHUTE BRAKE
- RADAR AND PERSONAL VIDEO SET
- NEXT MOVE PROGRAMMER
- POWDER SNOW MACHINE
- JET PACK
- THERMOSTATIC SKI SUIT
- TELESCOPIC/BINOCULAR SKI STICKS
- SNOW DEPTH FINDER
- MATE AND ANTI-MATE DEVICE
- FIRST AID
- SAFETY INFLATABLE CUSHION
- CASETTE TAPE RECORDER AND PLAYER
- FIENDISH RACE-POLE GRABS
- RUTTING IRONS
- POWDER SNOW CHUTES
- SKI JETS
- COMPUTER-CONTROLLED BINDINGS AND BOOTS
- PAIN-SENSING RELEASE MECHANISM
- LASER BEAM

Chapter Two: SKIER'S HIGHWAY CODE

HAVING EQUIPPED our skiers of the future in such a way as to ensure their greatest comfort and ultimate skiing success, let us now turn our attention to a most sadly neglected field—that of countering the numerous hazards and pitfalls that Mother Nature provides so that we might find skiing that bit more 'exciting'. We refer of course to the many trees, rocks, crevasses, dips, hollows and precipices which we are likely to encounter all too frequently in our skiing careers.

We may not of course necessarily be equipped with the skills and technique to do much about them, but we are suggesting that something in the way of warning signs, such as one sees littered all over our system of roads, should be provided. For those craving excitement, this will surely provide enough of the thrills of anticipation, and for the others of us, the vast majority, it will at least give us the chance to be in the best 'position' to deal with the inevitable disaster.

STEEP HILL

1:2

MAXIMUM
WIDTH
3 ft. 6 in.

3'6"

TWO-WAY TRAFFIC

OVERTAKING
SKI INSTRUCTOR
PROHIBITED

PISTE NARROWS

SLIPPERY PISTE

ROUTE DEVIATES
SHARPLY
TO RIGHT

END OF SPEED LIMIT

UNEVEN PISTE...

FALLING
SKIERS

BEWARE REINDEER

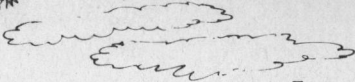

LOW FLYING SKIERS

HUMPBACK BRIDGE

EXPRESS
SKIWAY
No STOPPING!

SLOW
ACCIDENT

Chapter Three:

BASIC MANOEUVRES ON SKIS

Our New Revolutionary Method of Ski Instruction

THE AUTHORS have been of the opinion for many years that most troubles a skier will encounter in his skiing can be attributed directly to the over-complicated technique taught by his instructor.

Skiing is basically such a very easy sport, and we believe that the following illustrations should clarify and simplify the understanding of the basic forces involved in the art of manoeuvring a pair of skis.

STRAIGHT RUNNING

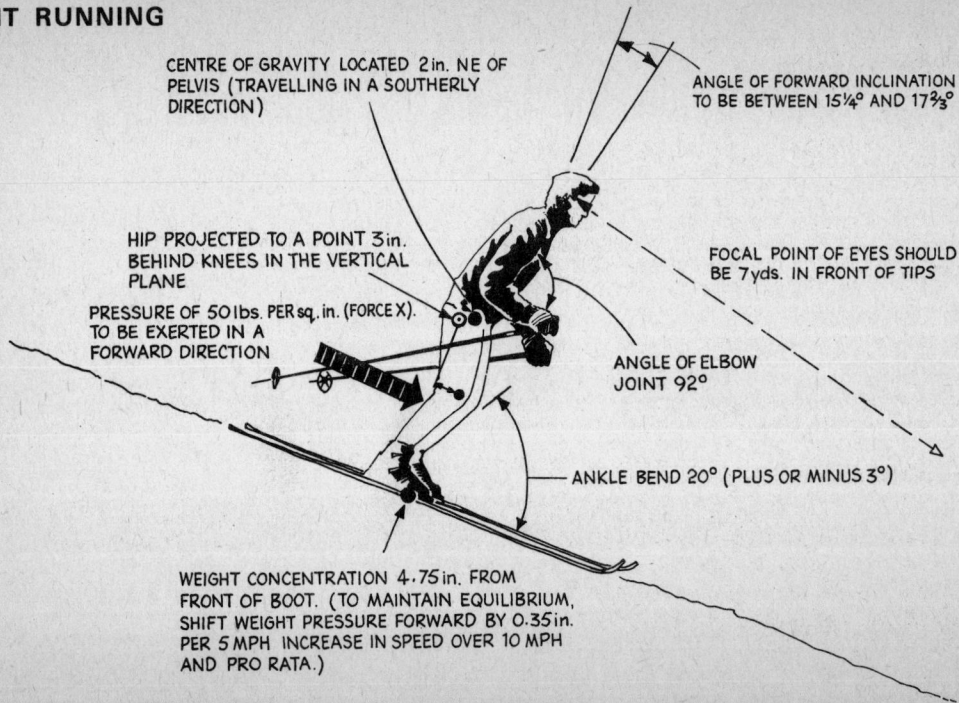

CENTRE OF GRAVITY LOCATED 2 in. NE OF PELVIS (TRAVELLING IN A SOUTHERLY DIRECTION)

ANGLE OF FORWARD INCLINATION TO BE BETWEEN 15¼° AND 17⅔°

HIP PROJECTED TO A POINT 3 in. BEHIND KNEES IN THE VERTICAL PLANE

FOCAL POINT OF EYES SHOULD BE 7 yds. IN FRONT OF TIPS

PRESSURE OF 50 lbs. PER sq. in. (FORCE X) TO BE EXERTED IN A FORWARD DIRECTION

ANGLE OF ELBOW JOINT 92°

ANKLE BEND 20° (PLUS OR MINUS 3°)

WEIGHT CONCENTRATION 4.75 in. FROM FRONT OF BOOT. (TO MAINTAIN EQUILIBRIUM, SHIFT WEIGHT PRESSURE FORWARD BY 0.35 in. PER 5 MPH INCREASE IN SPEED OVER 10 MPH AND PRO RATA.)

The most common deviation from the correct
position occurs when Force X is acting
backwards. When this happens you will
probably finish up looking like the normal
ski school beginner.

SNOW PLOUGH POSITION

THE ANGLE OF ARM BEND SHOULD BE
APPROX. 93° AND CENTRE OF
GRAVITY OF THE ARMS SHOULD
BE MAINTAINED WITHIN 18in.
(UPWARD ANGLE 18°
BACKWARD ANGLE 9°)
RELATIVE TO THE CENTRE
OF GRAVITY OF THE BODY,
GIVE OR TAKE 0.005in.

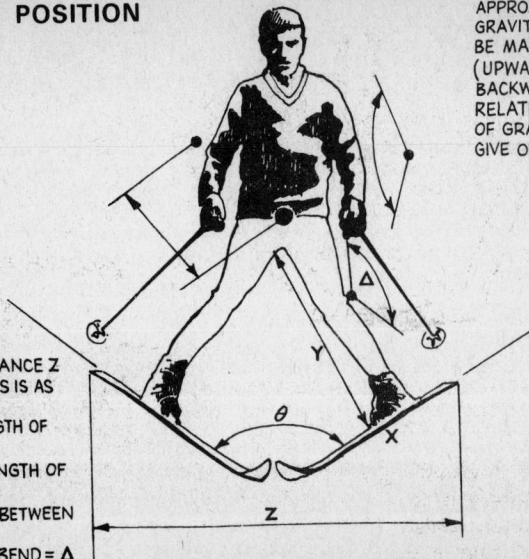

FORMULA TO FIND DISTANCE Z
BETWEEN BACKS OF SKIS IS AS
FOLLOWS :-
 WHERE 180 cms. LENGTH OF
 SKI = X
 WHERE 2ft. 9ins. LENGTH OF
 INSIDE LEG = Y
 WHERE 47° ANGLE BETWEEN
 SKI TIPS = θ
 WHERE 130° KNEE BEND = Δ

FOR 6ft.6in. SKIER ON 215 cms. SKIS :-

THUS $Z = \dfrac{2X - 145\,cms.}{Y2\,\dfrac{(\theta + \Delta)}{4}}$

When attempting to stop in the snow plough position, the most common mistake is to plant the poles in front of the ski tips whilst still moving. This will generally result in a rather too abrupt termination of forward velocity.

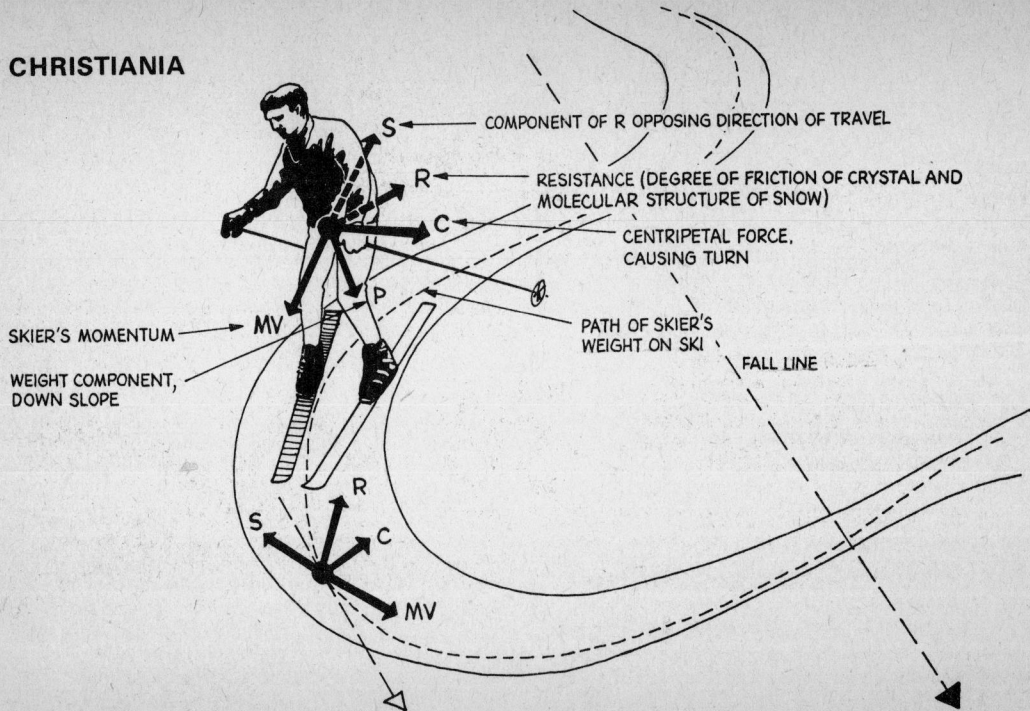

STEM CHRISTIANIA

S — COMPONENT OF R OPPOSING DIRECTION OF TRAVEL

R — RESISTANCE (DEGREE OF FRICTION OF CRYSTAL AND MOLECULAR STRUCTURE OF SNOW)

C — CENTRIPETAL FORCE, CAUSING TURN

SKIER'S MOMENTUM — MV

P — PATH OF SKIER'S WEIGHT ON SKI

WEIGHT COMPONENT, DOWN SLOPE

FALL LINE

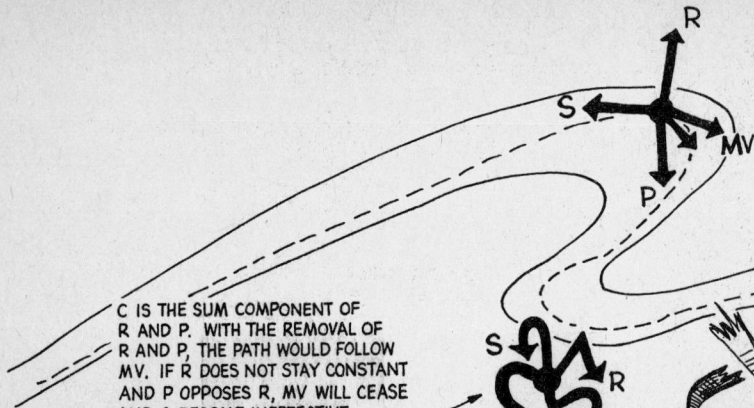

C IS THE SUM COMPONENT OF
R AND P. WITH THE REMOVAL OF
R AND P, THE PATH WOULD FOLLOW
MV. IF R DOES NOT STAY CONSTANT
AND P OPPOSES R, MV WILL CEASE
AND C BECOME INEFFECTIVE
THUS :–

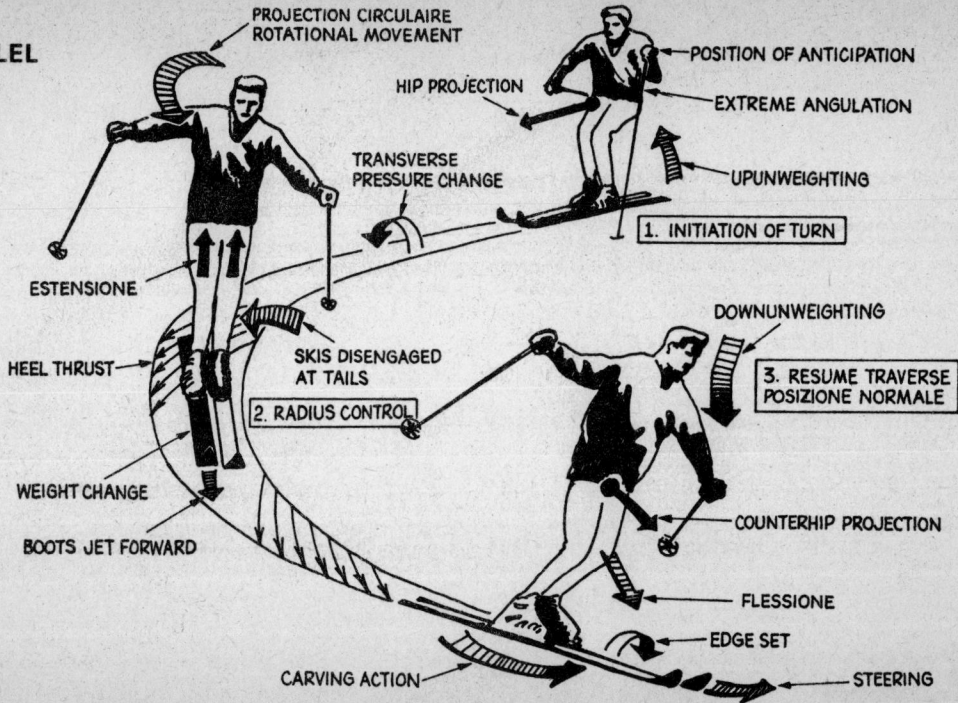

PARALLEL TURN

PROJECTION CIRCULAIRE
ROTATIONAL MOVEMENT

POSITION OF ANTICIPATION

HIP PROJECTION

EXTREME ANGULATION

TRANSVERSE
PRESSURE CHANGE

UPUNWEIGHTING

ESTENSIONE

1. INITIATION OF TURN

HEEL THRUST

SKIS DISENGAGED
AT TAILS

DOWNUNWEIGHTING

3. RESUME TRAVERSE
POSIZIONE NORMALE

2. RADIUS CONTROL

WEIGHT CHANGE

COUNTERHIP PROJECTION

BOOTS JET FORWARD

FLESSIONE

EDGE SET

CARVING ACTION

STEERING

This turn is usually achieved with ease by the well-endowed lady skiers. Too much *projection circulaire*, however, could cause a nasty accident!

1.

2.

3!

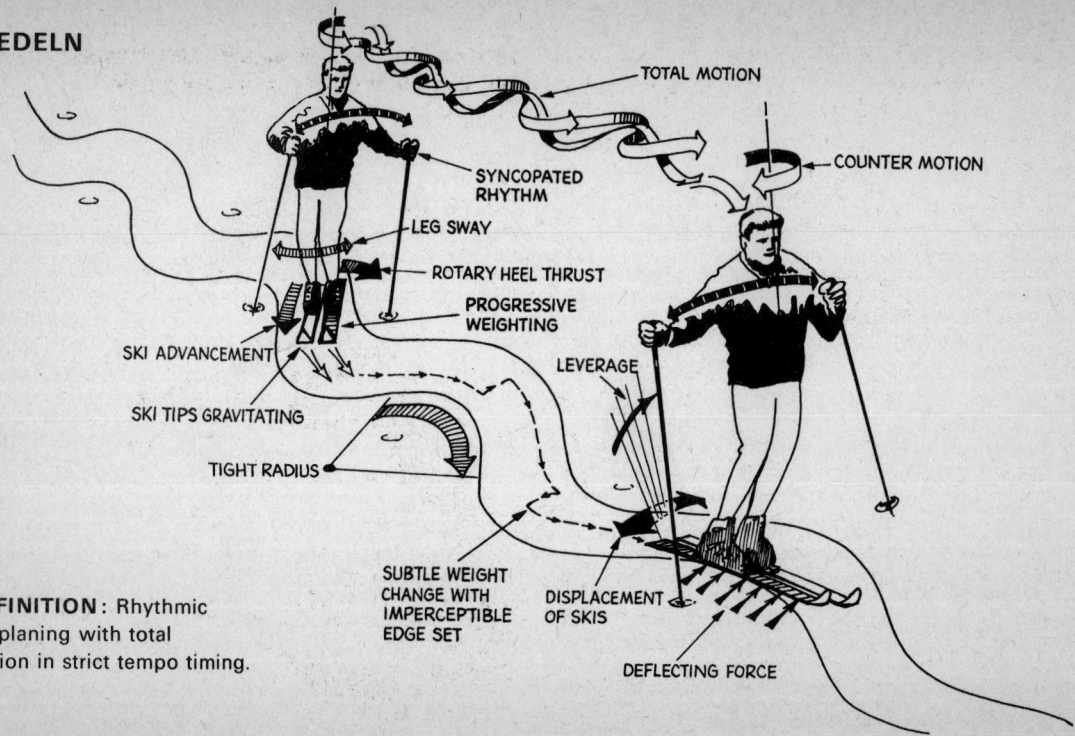

WEDELN

TOTAL MOTION

COUNTER MOTION

SYNCOPATED RHYTHM

LEG SWAY

ROTARY HEEL THRUST

PROGRESSIVE WEIGHTING

SKI ADVANCEMENT

LEVERAGE

SKI TIPS GRAVITATING

TIGHT RADIUS

SUBTLE WEIGHT CHANGE WITH IMPERCEPTIBLE EDGE SET

DISPLACEMENT OF SKIS

DEFLECTING FORCE

DEFINITION: Rhythmic leg planing with total motion in strict tempo timing.

Too fast a wedeln may result in attempting to turn in both directions at the same time.

Chapter Four: SKIING ONE-UPMANSHIP

LET'S FACE IT, we are never going to make good skiers. This in i'self is not important but what *does* matter is that our friends should think of us as being the type of skier one sees in all those glossy skiing magazines. This is simply a question of carefully preparing the right image for all situations.

Skiing begins with clothing, and here we can immediately assume the world-wide experienced skier image by sewing onto our anoraks as many little badges depicting the various top resorts that we can obtain.

SKI AIRLIFT
NEW ZEALAND
DAVOS
N. POLE
GLEN SKI
HAMPSTEAD HEATH
SKI ON SNOW
SUN VALLEY
SKI CLUB
SCOTLAND
COIRE CAS
USSR
MT. FUJI
Aspen
BP
SKI SCHOOL
FRED'S SKI SCHOOL
S. POLE
RED SNOW
KITZ
AROSA
St Moritz
PISTEY BEASTEY
SQUAW VALLEY
PLAYTEX
STOP
BEA
CHILE
St. Moritz

A sticker for our car, giving details of the next Winter Olympics, will immediately classify us as one of the leading lights of the sport.

THERE CAN be hardly anything more subtly designed to impress, than to be able to discuss all the many famous runs at the top resorts. We should therefore arm ourselves with a great vocabulary of famous runs, such as the Mattun or the Schindlerkar at St. Anton, the Mont Gelé at Verbier or perhaps the Corvatsch at St. Moritz, which we can trot out to our friends in casual conversation at the bar. It will impress them enormously to know that we once skied one of these great runs in seven foot of powder snow, on only one ski, (the tip of the other broke off, and the ski had to be discarded).

What actually happened

Another little snippet of conversation might be: '... I remember schussing down the North Wall of the Eiger to the Scheidegg ...'

What actually happened ...

'... by slightly mistiming my jump in the Innsbruck Olympics, I finished up in the top of this tree ...'

What actually happened ...

Another bar conversation piece which will give us immediate psychological superiority, is to be able to discuss the advantages and disadvantages of, say, the 'Avalement' technique.

This will require careful swotting up from a good ski book, but the result should definitely be worthwhile.

It should not normally be too difficult to steal an instructor's badge from somewhere. As well as getting priority on the ski lifts, one gets that wonderful heady feeling of being worshipped by every attractive female beginner on the slopes (night life no problem).

With only a little practice it is not difficult to learn to ski on just one ski. This should be done on the beginners' slopes to provide the maximum comparison with your own brilliance.

One manoeuvre certainly worth a little perfecting is the fast and abrupt *Christiania Stop*. When effected properly it is possible to shoot out a great shower of wet snow straight into the face of the nearest onlooker.

Perhaps the ultimate way of impressing other skiers is to march out on to the slopes with a huge bundle of slalom poles and wearing a crash helmet. The fact that one cannot do a snowplough turn is beside the point. It is only important to know the basic rudiments of setting a slalom course, and one can then stand there, stopwatch in hand, timing friends' pathetic attempts at this 'simple' run.

N CONCLUSION

If after reading this book you still cannot ski—never mind, you will be in good company! Why not take up golf . . . ?